Songs from the Shaper's Harp

poems by

Roberta Schultz

Finishing Line Press
Georgetown, Kentucky

Songs from the Shaper's Harp

Copyright © 2017 by Roberta Schultz
ISBN 978-1-63534-317-5 First Edition
All rights reserved under International and Pan-American Copyright Conventions.
No part of this book may be reproduced in any manner whatsoever without written permission from the publisher, except in the case of brief quotations embodied in critical articles and reviews.

ACKNOWLEDGMENTS

"Forbidden Fruit" was published in *Kudzu*, 2015
"High Wire" was published in *Still: the Journal, Winter*, 2016
"Perspective" was published in *Pine Mountain Sand & Gravel: Appalachia Under Thirty, Volume 19*, 2016
I am ever grateful for all thin places like Wildacres Retreat Center and Montreat. I cherish the circles that inspired and helped to craft these poems: Pauletta Hansel's "Practice of Poetry," Thomas More College's Creative Writing Vision, Southern Appalachian Writer's Cooperative, Appalachian Writers' Workshop at Hindman, and Greater Cincinnati Writers' League.

Publisher: Leah Maines

Editor: Christen Kincaid

Cover Art: Ebeth Scott Sinclair

Author Photo: Donna Campbell

Cover Design: Elizabeth Maines McCleavy

Printed in the USA on acid-free paper.
Order online: www.finishinglinepress.com
   also available on amazon.com

Author inquiries and mail orders:
Finishing Line Press
P. O. Box 1626
Georgetown, Kentucky 40324
U. S. A.

Table of Contents

Songs from the Shaper's Harp 1
Iona 2
20th Century Parenting 3
When I Don't Know What to Call Something 4
Forbidden Fruit 6
The Amazon Algorithm Plays Matchmaker 7
High Wire 8
Lesson 9
This is the Body of Water 10
Grass Carp: a Sestina 11
Clifford and Bobby Go Fishing 13
Morning Poem 14
He Returns 15
Left Hand 17
Messenger 18
How That Basket is Like My Mother 19
Night Song 21
Bird's Eye View 22
An Elegy for My Sadness 23
The Checklist 24
Carp 26
Rental Car 27
The Color of Mud 29
Perspective 30
Lullaby 31

Songs from the Shaper's Harp

He asks for a tune to fire the torches,
or a melody to pierce the shields
of speechless creatures who cower low
in underwater caves.

I pluck the strings to offer myths
of old gods, thunder, plunder,
rough seas and a lonely wanderer
whose wife kept watch from the highest cliff.

"Not that," he grumbles, draining his ale-cup,
slamming it down on the bare mead-bench.
"Not that." Shadows echo along the dim walls.
"Weave me a song that will break your heart."

I sing now of warriors who fight for the lost cause,
who leave arms and legs in the sand of far shores,
and of those who come home in one piece from the ends
of the ragged world, wailing for light like ghosts.

Iona*

    "It is an honest ghost, that let me tell you." —Hamlet, Act I, Scene 5

As the dream unfolds, we float in circles.
My sisters and I hug the bristly back
of a tawny ridge while the shoreline shifts.
Maybe we ride the spine of a creature
submerged. At the dock I slide off alone
for grandma's house where father sips coffee.
Through the haze of those nether rooms, Grandma
cups Daddy's face, "you are my favorite son."

Why has it been so long since I came here?

No plot too strange to stretch night's liquid veil—
the ghosts fade like mist, blue-green and swirling,
before they sing the isle's chorus—before
light prods the shadow beast back to the deep
where still I grip the island's sun-warmed mane.

*Iona is a sacred place in Scotland where the veil between this world and the next is believed to be thin.

20th Century Parenting

The little adult raises two parents and two
siblings on her nickel-a-day allowance.
She slogs off to work each morning
at the brick schoolyard, finger painting

songs on wood blocks, sweating it out
at hopscotch and four square. When the bell rings
at 3 pm, she rushes back to Grandma's kitchen,
scrubbing the chrome-edged table,

mixing pudding and cornbread for evening meals where
parents slouch nodding at their plates, worn out from their day
of pulling shoe boxes from high perches. Unsold soles haunt
their dreamy conversation as the little adult slides coffee

past their tweedy elbows, passes Rainbow bread and butter
toward her scowling Grandpa who is already unwrapping
his first Ibold, preparing to puff smoke and politics across
that table to all challengers who enter the fray, giddy for battle:

teenage aunt with a high school vocabulary, unemployed
uncle, a loner with war injuries we don't discuss.
Shoe salesmen parents suddenly awake at their plates,
ready to defend or attack who is or who is not Catholic,

who is or who is not Republican while the grandparents—
whose rental house they all live in—circle the table, slamming
down pudding bowls in front of each place setting. Clattering
Fire King and rattling spoons, scattering those "seen and not heard,"

pudding bowls tucked low, out the screen door
toward the front stoop where little adults become
children, play-suited and pig-tailed, sisters
giggling over the kitchen din.

When I Don't Know What to Call Something

I call it salad.

Violet says it can't be that because there isn't lettuce.
She has that one definition in her brain.
I can't talk it out of her.

Yet, pretzels, red Jello, and strawberries refuse to combine
or blend. They persist in being themselves suspended, offering
juxtaposed tastes—three dimensional, separate, tossed—

if you will, or if you won't. The dictionary—that 20th Century oracle
we drew like swords when Grandpa invented a word for double score
in Scrabble—settles it. But she uses an app

that backs up what I already know for sure—otherwise I'd
never go to the mat. Everyone should know that about me
after all this time. I admit mistakes.

Only now will I seek the higher source—
Webster's Seventh New Collegiate.
Only now will I face my own certainty
on parchment pages, not unlike *King James.*

There it is under definition "b."

Gelatin—a possible ingredient.

By coincidence, my e-mail chimes
to remind me of a new message
for the inbox. Subject Line:

WOW YOUR GUESTS WITH SHOW-STOPPING SALAD.

Electronic objects around me
are somehow detecting my thoughts.
Last week the TV repeated my words out loud.

I have witnesses. Most people would call
them reliable. Is it possible that algorithms—like
viruses that jump species—can heat-seek firing synapses?

"Salad," I say loudly to tempt fate.

The dull sounds of a soap opera rumble from the living room.
No one echoes my word. I cannot make it happen on purpose.

Forbidden Fruit

One slice, and a pale half moon
wobbles in vortex
to the center of the
service.

Then, fingertips sprinkle
a sweet blessing
on the golden bowl of
rind.

Spoon carves each juicy pink section
in ritual triangles, lifting
sweet-sour flesh to
tongue.

Grandma's brown hands offer
turquoise Melmac cup.
Perfume of first coffee, like incense.
Crunch of dark toast.
Prepare the gifts of
breakfast.

Hands, still.
Cups, lost to yard sales.
Coffee, blacker now.
Toast, lighter.

Mint green pill
placed on my tongue
by the order of serpent and staff.
I take it as atonement for my sin,
cholesterol.

The Amazon Algorithm Plays Matchmaker

First comes a love note
pairing Old Blue Eyes
with Taylor Swift's *1989*.
Frank chimes in next
with *A Swinging Affair*.

I remind him under my breath
that he is old enough
to be her second great-grandfather.

"All About that Bass,"
he snaps back, using
the next suggested title
to assert his Chairman status.

"You Know I'm No Good,"
growls Amy Winehouse
from the sidelines (featuring
Ghostface Killah.)

Frank meets her sultry parry
with his *Greatest Hits*.

Never mind, *1989*.
Frank and Amy lock
smoky lungs in a 1960s
cocktail lounge—all bossa nova
moans and shadowy eyes.

Ghostface Killah scurries
off to the end of the line
where Pentatonix challenges
him to a beatbox throw down.

I want to tell the algorithm
that I bought Sinatra for my
91-year-old mother-in-law.
But why spoil the party?

High Wire (after May Sarton's "An Observation")

Some players cannot bear
finger picks between the soft
pluck and the resonating

string. Tips wear blisters, dance
liquid sacrifice over fretboard, caressing
warm bronze, never scraping or buzzing

angel breath from triads. I dodge
the sound man's slings, duck
thumb picker's arrows. They would hoist

shields—bright clang of metal
on metal. Wounded digits sense
their way to truth. Daredevils inching

over taut steel.
They feel the way,
never looking down.

Lesson

Like Tarzan in leopard skin
I swam underwater, free.

Mom and Aunt Marge paddled like
dogs, their heads above surface.

To teach me how to survive,
those traitors tossed me in the

deep end. I gasp for air still.

This Is the Body of Water

I was baptized in the dark silty dregs
of York Street School's public pool.
In just five black inches of leafy sludge, I plunged
in my golden houndstooth Easter coat.

Much later I practiced
the joys of communal bath—
three sisters in a tub on Sunday nights
to save holy water from the cistern.

I received first communion
in summer downpours, spinning
liturgical dance in my underwear—
sacred drops on outstretched tongue.

Rededicating my life to rescue
clowning children from eternal horseplay,
I returned to pools where I worshipped
another lifeguard, thinking him a sun god—

though we blew the same whistles,
knew the same cross chest carry.

Forsaking all bodies, I fell prostrate
on the sand before the ocean,
Waves washed me clean, ordained my toes
with starfish and tide pools.

In darker nights, I grasped the rocks
near Lake Superior, clutched the stony slant
of Mers Les Bains. From cliffs I witnessed
angels ascending from the beach.

I will take last rites on a quiet lake where bass rise.
Where once I heard them sing.

Grass Carp: a Sestina

Iridescent scales of color
shimmer in the wake of marauding grass carp.
As they travel in schools of size,　　one
leader stirs the shallow yellow mud
where sudden turns launch a line
of torpedoes toward the center of the lake's still

point. There they stir the surface, stillness
rippled by dorsal fins. Devouring colored
honey suckle blossoms, wide mouths line
out the lack of duckweed and grass clippings, carping
at low-hanging sycamore branches to slide through the mud,
and fill their ritual gaping.　　One

plastic bobber dangles from the shag bark. Once
you might have cast a dough ball in the still
green pool under that tree near the muddy
bank, a hook gleaming under red and white colors.
thinking you could land a twenty-five pound carp.
But you have witnessed snapping lines,

broken rods, and empty nets of fishermen who line
the dam, trusting their own tackle.　　One
second before a lure lands, sleek carp
submerge like stealthy submarines. Still
evading sly herons in camouflage colored
hats, they dive toward cool mud.

On a bright afternoon with no breeze and no mud,
I watch from the end of the dock as lines
of shadows glide beneath deep blue and white—colors
echoing the sky's dome.　　One
crashing whale breaks the mirror's glassy stillness,
emerging from the lake to snatch a frond of cat tail. Another carp

flings itself at a low stem of elderberry, clenching a leaf. These carp
are White Amur, bred to eat grass, not to hide in mud
on the lake's bottom. I've watched for floating stillness
near the lake's overflow. They rarely take the bait from weightless lines.
In twenty years I've found just   one
lifeless, scales blazing a spectrum of royal color.

I scooped that floating carp into a long-handled net, coloring
my face red with effort, my hand streaking mud from one
arm leaning into water. Above, the trees still decked with ruined fishing
line.

Clifford and Bobby Go Fishing

In the story Grandpa told

you sit in the front
of the canoe on Dietz's Lake, talking
about God-knows-what
over limburger and cans of Wiedemann.

You wear that go-to-hell hat, decidedly Russian,
lamb black with ear flaps, as you stand in the bow
smiling and shading your eyes.

Then, lifting one yellow rubber boot
to the bench, you proclaim,
"Lafayette, we are here!"

As your arms swing wide to greet
imaginary Normans on a beach, Grandpa
seizes the forgotten paddle.

Surprised grinning walrus,
you gasp to the leafy surface,
bangs and mustache dripping,
wire rims dangling from one ear.

Morning Poem

They float like beads
of oil from a tanker, bubbling
up on Pacific waves in rainbows.

They disappear like diamonds
of sweat brushed by rough knuckles
from the brow of concentration.

They choke me with tight
clasps, these words.
These necklaces.

He Returns

1. On this high hill I wait at sunset
after the clock falls back and the dark
slinks in like a panther on its belly,
stretching toward the woods.

At this hour, sirens wail duets
near the Licking below at Double A.
There, cars and trucks pound rapids
echoing through the canyon cut by 275.

One hawk patrols the pines
at lake's edge.

2. Did she wait all those years
on a cliff near the rough open seas
while the pink mouth of horizon
swallowed each sun?

In those hours, sirens crooned
shanties, luring sailors toward
sharp reefs of disaster, rocking
the waiting with lullabies, toneless and endless.

One gull leaned—keening through the masts—
into cold north wind.

3. Here, near this still lake
we huddle around fire that feeds
on the dried ash logs of our dreams,
on the shag bark kindling of our nightmares.

In this moment, a thin slice of moon
sickles the ripples of black mirror.
One toad trills a litany for November.
A bat soundlessly bombards the waves.

The great horned owl moans
against icy stars

Left Hand

I watch it carelessly
stroke the dog's thick
mantel, twisting yellow-brown
coyote hair between
long calloused digits

that used to finger chords
on a Martin D35, thump
bass notes on a Fender.

Still, that left hand crooks
two bottles of beer from the fridge
on Fridays, stuffs the *chiminea*
with pine boughs, somehow
manages to strike a match
against an ash log, stokes
the fire by shag bark limb, insists
on holding the leash while I caper
in zigzags toward
the lake, unencumbered.

I twirl the carved walking
stick in both hands
like a baton, marching
five steps ahead.

Hanging from the wrist
in a stiff grip,
his right hand brushes
loose rhythm
against denim.

Messenger

There are days when the Universe dips
in with some hint of insight,

and you don't know where you stashed
that red plastic scoop—

the one for gathering inspiration from the heap
of accumulating nonsense.

In the freezer you find a slab of bagged
ice requiring a three-foot drop onto concrete

or—at the very least—a hammer from the junk
drawer of useful tools you harbor while

right in front of your dazzled mind, silver liquid
hardens into a pile of sharp-edged gems,

each jewel threatening to melt if you can't fashion
a deft vessel from your shivering hands.

How That Basket is Like My Mother

I. Basket

Across the room sleeps
something familiar.
Brown patterns like diamonds
on a Navajo rug.

Just another roadside attraction
sold under a bower on a desert road.
A souvenir for your mantel
that stows earrings
away from pawing curiosity
of cat claws.

Or maybe a basket for secrets,
folded and sealed inside.
Secured by silky wisps of twine,
the snug lid fools prying eyes
with a seamless weave.

II. Mother

When I ask her what
she had for breakfast,
she can't recall.
But she brushes away imaginary
crumbs in a ritual movement
near her mouth.
"Your hair is so curly!"
She smiles in surprise,
as if seeing me for the first time.
I kiss her cheek.

III. Basket

Smell sweetgrass, taste sage.
Caress gnarled knots.
Loops of memory overlapping sinew.
Geometric stacking of the tiny stem.
A tight core of stitching stretches
four directions, anchoring the base.

IV. Mother

"There's no place like home,"
she sings in a low voice as I
wheel her into the living room.
"Queen Anne's Lace along the highway,"
she remembers a line
my sister wrote.

V. Basket and Mother

Universes revealed
in pear shape.
Acorns storing up mysteries
for future oaks.

The stories coiled inside
rise only for music of the spheres.
Never again charmed
by dark-haired men
with cedar songs.

Night Song

At night, I sing with my mother's voice.
A keen somewhere between
moaning hound and surprised parrot
parts my cracked lips.

I wake myself with groaning
known only to those
opening a door,
answering a phone,
or pulling back a curtain
on cold truths that
shudder in the dark.

Bird's Eye View

Because I want to believe in
  eventually,
I walk the pilgrim path of
  gradually,
Shuffling over rough stones of
  daily
to help choose the urn.

Today I drive past the nursing home,
  remembering how I once witnessed
    a cardinal spiraling down to the road.

His stunned father lay slain
  at the crosswalk, in the wake
    of a rumbling garbage truck.

Between cars, a son whorls
  down, down, down to white paint
    fanning lifeless feathers with red urging.

An Elegy for My Sadness

I sing this song, the one
I know by heart.

For her sighs, drawn out
in long vowel chorus.

For her tears, the copper
aftertaste of disappointment.

For her slow, dragging steps away
from sun on her skin, I sing:

The gospel train is coming,
and don't you want to go
and leave this world of trials
and trouble here below?*

She hums along distracted
through the long hallways
of dusty breath, barely noticing
the bright high windows,
the open door.

**From "Talk About Suffering" —a traditional song*

The Checklist

"Why not teach her the 23rd?" Mom leans half-way
out the door on her way to work at Schiff's Shoes.

"Because everyone knows that one." Daddy lifts
me up on the table next to the checklist.

He waits, arms crossed,
as I sing in a little bird voice:

"The earth is the lord's and the fullness thereof." The next
line has bigger, harder words. I take a breath.

"For he hath founded it upon the seas
and established it upon the floods."

He combs my hair, then checks the chart.
Teeth brushed. Check.
Face and hands washed in the tiny basin. Check.

Shoes tied. Shoes tied. Shoes tied.
After three attempts, I make the final loop. Check.

Navy blue sailor dress, the very best
I have. Half pony tail sagging to the left.

One large front tooth juxtaposed
against a new one breaking gum.

Picture day. Extra care. Daddy booms
the next line as a challenge:

"Who shall ascend unto the hill of the lord
and who shall stand in his holy place?"

"He who hath not sworn deceitfully?"
I ask, uncertain.

He stops to trace the line with his finger
in the worn brown copy of *Readings from the Holy
Scriptures for Jewish Soldiers and Sailors*. Then nods.

"He who hath clean hands and a pure heart."
He inspects my fingernails for grime.

Dropping my hands, he continues,
"This is the generation who seek after him."

"Who seek thy name, O, Jacob!"
I remember, smiling.

"Lift up your heads, o ye gates
and be ye lifted up ye everlasting doors
that the king of glory may come in."
Daddy says this in a sing-song.

"Who is this king of glory?" we ask in unison.

I begin to chant and clap my answer:
"The lord strong and mighty.
The lord mighty in battle."

Daddy tilts his forehead against mine
and looks over his glasses:
"Who is this king of glory?"

"The lord of hosts. He is the king of glory."
I pronounce this dramatically, feeling the line drop.

He hoists me from the table,
pressing the grooming checklist
into my satchel,
folding word rhythms
between pockets of time.

Carp

> "Who would there fardels bear
> to grunt and sweat under a weary life." —Hamlet, Act III, Scene 1

Grey puffs echo toward open blue
  where grass carp seem to swim through hoops
    skimming thick duckweed off tips of clouds.

As Uncle Billy blows bold smoke rings
in her face, Granda Babe scolds,
"all you do is carp."

"Carp! Carp! Carp!" A fishwife understands sea change.
"Pluck! Pluck! Pluck" Conquering Romans command.
"Brag! Brag! Brag!" Ancient Norsemen boast.

What muddy ponds of meaning do they stir?
Like beards on fish—
sharp barbels.

Like drums: "Carp, carp, carp!"
Ancestor mumblings plunder my ears,
channeled into songs from the deep

by the air
by the pen
by the tongue.

They must be carried,
these word bundles left behind.
Bear these fardels.

Rental Car

It's that exotic sliding into something that's
not really mine
feeling.

The lingering cologne of air freshener to make
me think that no one ever smoked inside
this sleek animal crouching
so low to the ground.

I'm dizzy from the purring engine
that only growls when climbing
mountain roads,
hugging the curves the way my
utility-minded SUV could never
imagine.
Never tilting.
Lunging deftly with taut muscles
over sun-dappled
gravel toward
the pinnacle.

The trunk, a treasure chest
of empty,
hiding my water bottle for
a week in crevices
so remote, my fingers ache for
time to explore.

Something about the smooth
black seats, the 20th Century clock
with hands, the silver deco emblem
stretching across the steering wheel,
lures me toward a
rendezvous with endless
highways

free from baggage, scrapes, claims,
history of any kind.

Only the odometer clicks off
merchant miles others spent
in the embrace of this
shiny beast.

The CD player takes on
one customer at a time.
Forcing me to slow down,
hold on, enjoy the ride,
and sing.

The Color of Mud
  (A Ghazal)

Peepers sing in the color of mud.
Turtles spring from the color of mud.

Black loam churned for the four o' clocks.
Seed planting in the color of mud.

Pine needles shower the red dirt road.
Wind whistling for the color of mud.

Cracked dry mouth of a yellow stream.
Clay throat gasping for the color of mud.

Harbor sinks at the Leland Dock.
The whole town dredging for the color of mud.

Pale, pocked face of the lonely moon
still pining for the color of mud.

She chooses a sweater from the Goodwill rack
never noticing it's the color of mud.

Perspective

The Italian man in coveralls paints a mural
of Wiedemann's Fine Beer on Volz's Market.
He leans three stories up on nothing but
a ladder, blue rag bulging from back pocket.

I watched his progress after school from 12th
and Columbia. Monday, just the base
of goblet beaded with sweat. Friday's rise—
Bohemian lager cresting to foam head.

How can it look so real this far away
when the painter stands only bubbles tall?
His beer glass towers almost three flights high.
White swell drizzles over the thin glass rim.

Fresh golden whorls smoothed over crumbling brick.
This *Starry Night*, a sky for thirsty work.

Lullaby: a Translation Poem
(after Erica Konya's "Prodigal")

Often singing alone
in the woods
opens a wide space, so wide
it feels dissonant
particularly if
you keep pressing
part of the song
to stay inside
when no one else appears
to weave a harmony
through its humble
quivering threads or to murmur:
     my own
and
     hush now sweet
     and gentle throat
yet soon (slowly to croon)
soft echoes
breathe a lullaby
your voice becomes the mother
your voice becomes the child

Roberta Schultz plays guitar, sings, and writes for the Kentucky women's trio, Raison D'Etre who have 9 recordings and one live concert DVD to their credit. They are adjudicated to Kentucky's Performing Arts Directory since 2000. Her song lyrics "January Thaw" and "The Papers" are published in two *Motif* (Motes Books) anthologies edited by poet, Marianne Worthington. While two of her songs made it to the second round of judging in the Great American Songwriting Contest, "Sure Thing" was a 2013 finalist. Her song, "Broken Radio," was awarded Judge's Choice in the Mountain Valley Arts Songwriting Competition, judged by Pierce Pettis. After attending the SoLaTiDo Songwriting Retreat in North Carolina for many years, Schultz completed her first solo album of original songs, *One Small Step*, with Richard Putnam of Big Feat Productions on keyboards, accompanying and arranging. She also published her first chapbook of poetry in 2014 with Finishing Line Press.

Schultz is a regular contributor of book reviews to *Around Cincinnati*, a culture and arts program that airs each Sunday on NPR affiliate, WVXU, produced by longtime Cincinnati jazz and blues host, Lee Hay. She currently lives in Wilder, KY with her husband, Gary, dog, Maggie, and cat, Ruthie.

www.ingramcontent.com/pod-product-compliance
Lightning Source LLC
LaVergne TN
LVHW041508070426
835507LV00012B/1423